Lord Byron's Foot

POEMS

George Green

WINNER OF THE NEW CRITERION POETRY PRIZE

St. Augustine's Press
SOUTH BEND, IN 2012

Funding for this year's New Criterion Poetry Prize
has been provided by Joy & Michael Millette

Library of Congress Cataloging-in-Publication Data:

Green, George Wayne, 1950–
    Lord Byron's foot: poems / George Green
        p. cm
    "Winner of the New Criterion Poetry Prize."
    ISBN 978-1-58731-477-3 (clothbound: acid-free paper)
    I. Title
    PS3557.R3717L67 2012
    811'.54 — c23   2012042346

Contents

For Marianne

Acknowledgments

JOURNALS
American Arts Quarterly, "The Treaty of Paris."
Barrow Street, "Sirius."
Court Green, "The Searchers."
Fulcrum, "The People in Hopper's Paintings."
Good Foot, "Little Cross," "Tarzan and the Leopard Woman."
Hanging Loose, "Stephen Duck and Edward Chicken," "Art Movies."
Inverval(le)s, "Warhol's Portraits."
Maggy, "Lord Byron's Foot."
Margie, "My Uncle's Bible."
Mississippi Review, "Broad Stripes and Bright Stars."
The New Criterion, "Poor Collins," "Rose Poe," "The Death of Winckelmann."
River Styx, "Ronell Laborde."
Smithsonian, "Confederates Try to Burn New York."

ANTHOLOGIES
The Best American Poetry 2006, "The Death of Winckelmann."
The Best American Poetry 2005, "The Searchers."
Bright Wings: An Illustrated Anthology of Poems about Birds, "The Magnificent Frigatebird."
180 More: Extraordinary Poems for Every Day, "Stephen Duck and Edward Chicken."
Poetry 180: A Turning Back to Poetry, "The Portuguese in Mergui."
The Swallow Anthology of New American Poets, "The Death of Winckelmann," "My Uncle's Bible," "Stephen Duck and Edward Chicken," "Warhol's Portraits."

I would like to thank Diane Collins, Chris Calhoun, Kevin Cooney, and nature's nobleman, Paul Violi. My first workshops were conducted by William Pitt Root, and I will always remember his generosity. John Potter taught me to love Milton and Spenser. Thanks to Linda Gregg for the many dinners with Jack. Tim Steele and Dick Davis have been my guides and masters, and Joshua Mehigan is "the better craftsman."

Lord Byron's Foot

The Portuguese in Mergui

Without you I am like the Portuguese in Mergui,
who have forgotten their language
but still go to church,
unlike their surly neighbors, the Salon pirates,
who live near the mudbanks
trading pearls for opium.

Without you I am a geopolitical feature,
like Lot's wife, who only turned her head
like a doe in the forest
to watch the flaming city
crackle and poof.

Without you I must wait in this neglected park alone,
and though I might need a shoeshine
my bright red sport jacket
lends me the prominence of a woodpecker
and the authority of a rooster.

Without you I have brung a cupcake
for the birthday of Chester Nimitz,
who, reared among the dry hills of Texas,
far from any sea shore,
rose to command the mightiest armada
in the history of the world.

And am I not myself an admiral of the clouds?
As such I now command you to come home.

Warhol's Portraits

Liz

Marilyn killed herself because she thought
that middle age began at thirty-five.
In Liz's case it did, but she kept going,
though Dick went down in flames (*Exorcist II*).
This print's from '65 and she looks ready
to frug the night away with Peter Lawford,
who hasn't started wearing beads (not yet).
Those were the days, before the TV movies,
before the Percoset and Häagan Dazs.
Oblivious to the telltale signs, she smiles,
the long descent to Neverland begun.

Mick Jagger

He is in my opinion past his prime
already in this print, and he and Keith
are fast becoming tacky little skanks
and sherry-slurping, chicken-headed whores.
They shake their butts and sweat in leather pants,
like ancient drag queens high on Angel dust.

Dennis Hopper

His cowboy Hamlet death scenes are the best.
He flops, jerks, and blabs beseechingly,
then flops, imploringly, and dies. John Wayne,
even, is stunned by so much hamminess.
(He kills him twice: *True Grit* and *Katie Elder*.)
Now Dennis sells investments on TV
blabbing away to boomers who have bucks
enough to golf all day, enough to die
of boredom in the sun. Dennis is cool, though,
and still the hippest actor on the scene.
A poet and a painter, and, what's more,
a recognized authority on Andy.

Goethe

From Tischbein's portrait of the noble poet
lounging beside a shattered obelisk.
The campiness of Goethe's hat and cloak
no doubt explains why Andy did this copy.
The coloring is pure Electric Circus
and Maharishi-era Donovan.
"The savoring of unintended ironies"
is Peter Schjeldahl in last week's New Yorker
explaining camp to dopes out in the burbs.

Deborah Harry

She is expressionless, or nearly so,
and yet the muffled insolence is there,
a look that prom queens have—the secret stoners;
a look that cover girls will overdo.
I've seen that look on Bombay prostitutes
in coffee-table books, but, some of them,
pathetically, look out at us with hope,
as if a photograph could rescue them
or set them up inside a better cathouse.

Truman Capote

Those A-list types who had rejected Andy
(Capote, Rauschenberg, and Jasper Johns)
all came around when he got really big,
though friendship had become extraneous.
The portraits of his friends are extra flat.
You can't look into them: There is no in.
A frightful vacancy and transience
is what, I guess, he meant us all to see.
He might as well have kept on painting shoes.

Jerry Hall

I could step back and make a case for these,
regard them, somehow, in another light.
Maybe the sitters have been divinized
and that's why they all fade into abstraction.
Maybe those patches where the colors smear,
blurring the lines, express the soul's diffuse
ethereality, reminding us
of what, time and again, the Lord enjoins—
that we behold each other as divine.

Mao

The Chairman's constipation was so bad,
he only defecated once a week,
and during the Long March his weekly voidings
were sometimes celebrated by his troops.
Mao moved his bowels once on a mountaintop
above the clouds, and members of his staff
began to dance and clap their hands. The news
spread rapidly as cheers went up along
the mountainside. The tattered ranks rejoiced,
ten-thousand hats were tossed into the air!
From goat trails near the summit bugles sounded,
and acclamations echoed in the dells.

Sirius

Often on winter nights the only star
I see is Sirius, piercing the gloom
and glare from nearly nine light-years away.

So it's the star I have to wish upon.
One grim Pinocchio, here in Manhattan,
gazing up through the window of my garret.

The ancients were afraid. They thought the star
could kill their cows. Signore Dryden sings:
"If David's rule Jerusalem displease

the Dog Star heats their brains to this disease,"
and none of us wants that. Priam compares
the Dog Star to impetuous Achilles,

who dragged unhappy Hector through the dust.
But those were summer days, you must remember,
and Sirius was ruddier back then.

Tonight it's just a melancholy beam,
a loose bulb on the drunkard's porch that flickers,
a flashlight in the frozen climber's hand.

The People in Hopper's Paintings

It seems to me that all they do is loaf
and sit in torpid vacancy, adrift
within themselves. If only they'd go bowling
or hike around the reservoir and stop
staring portentously into the void
like baffled existentialists or Buddhists

in college towns. They really need TV
it seems. Without it they just lollygag
in solar-heated rooms or on the porch,
squinting into the glare at God knows what.
That guy whose face is buried in a pillow
may well have lost the will to live, or maybe

he's had his fill of living without drapes
or blinds or window shades of any kind
like everybody else in Hoppersville.
Those girls malingering in hotel lobbies,
reading *Tobacco Road* or *Lorna Doone*,
believe me, they're not going anywhere,

and Rudolf Valentino couldn't get
the time of day from them. They all just sit
there like stuffed animals in flapper hats,
brimming with crass expectancy, or sinking
in dull regret. In well lit parlor cars
they're even more stuck up, as each *displays*

a randomness of individual
concerns. So please don't kid yourself about
that naked lady smoking in the sunlight.
She's just a mental patient, not a nympho,
and after she has had her medication
they'll put her in the window like a plant.

Lord Byron's Foot

That day you sailed across the Adriatic,
wearing your scarlet jacket trimmed in gold,
you stood there on the quarter deck, beglamored,
but we were all distracted by your foot.
Your foot, your foot, your lordship's gimpy foot,
your twisted, clubbed and clomping foot, your foot.

Well, Caroline went half-mad for your love,
but did she ever try to make you dance?
No, never, never, never would that happen;
no, never with your limping Lordship's foot—
your foot, your foot, your lame and limping foot,
your limp and lumbering, plump and plodding foot.

We see you posing with your catamite,
a GQ fashion-spread from 1812,
but one shoe seems to differ from the other.
Is that the shoe that hides your hobbled foot?
Your foot, your foot, your game and gimping foot,
your halt and hobbled, clumped and clopping foot.

And why did Milbanke sue you for divorce?
T'was buggery? I really do doubt that.
It was your foot, and everybody knows it.
It's all we think about—your stupid foot.
Your foot, your foot, your clumsy, clumping foot,
your limp and gimping, stupid, stubby foot.

And after you had swum the Hellesponte,
"A fin is better than a foot," they'd say.
Behind your back they'd say, "a fin is better,"
meaning your Lordship's foot was just a fin.
A fin, a fin, your foot was just a fin;
your flubbed and flumping foot was just a fin.

And when you went to Cavalchina, masked,
with Leporello's list (only half male),
what were your friends all whispering about?
What had they been remembering—your foot?
Your foot, your foot, your halt and hampered foot.
Your hobbled, clubbed and clopping foot, your foot.

When Odevaere drew you on your deathbed,
with laurel on your alabaster brow,
he threw a blanket on your legs—but why?
Could it have been to cover up your foot?
Your foot, your foot, your pinched and palsied foot,
your crimped and clumping, gimped, galumphing foot.

It's best if we just contemplate your bust,
a bust by Thorvaldson or Bartolini,
and why is that you ask, and why is that?
So no one has to see your friggin' foot,
your foot, your foot, your clomping monster foot,
your foot, your foot, your foot, your foot, your foot!

Art Movies

Lust for Life

I learned how artists act from *Lust for Life*.
(That movie where Kirk Douglas plays Van Gogh.)
Refuse to get a job. That's how you start.
And then you have to mutilate yourself,
of course. How else could decent art be made,
or even contemplated?
                              Cut off your nose,
cut off your face,
                    drink coffee all day long,
and if the crows keep cawing in the corn,
just shoot yourself, and that will shut them up.
I learned a lot; I knew I was an artist.
But critics thought the movie was just kitsch.

How could you play that fag? Duke Wayne asked Kirk.

Rembrandt

Quoting the King James Version, constantly,
he's someone that you just can't help respecting.
And Gertrude Lawrence is in this!
Too bad
she didn't live to do *The King and I*
on film, for after all, the *I* was written
for her. But she'd have been too old by then,
and Deborah Kerr was prettier and younger.
Kerr would have got the part, I can assure you.
Younger and prettier is always better,
especially at the Met, where really hot
and slender cute sopranos rule this year.
In poetry, as well, it's obvious—
The girls are chosen for their jacket photos;
The guys all look as if they sang in hip
And groovy bands.
But Rembrandt's models—No!
They just ain't hot, especially Saskia.

How sweet that he is played by Charles Laughton.
Maybe too sweet.
How kind was Rembrandt, really?
He wouldn't loan me money, I don't think,
and I'd have helped him, gladly, if I could.
He knew vicissitudes. He calmed himself.
He painted Jesuses we can believe in.

The Agony and the Ecstasy

I learned a lot from this one, too. You have
to wreck, completely, your first fresco. Next,
you head up to the mountain top and see
the Sistine Chapel ceiling in the clouds,
and then—you're on your back in agony.
The ecstasy is when the Pope goes back
to bed. "When will you finish it?" He asks
a million times, "When will you finish it?"

Charlton, way up there on the scaffolding,
painting with chocolate pudding, so that when
it falls into his mouth it's pleasurable.
You're fine with this, except you don't like Charlton.
A charioteer, okay, a genius, no.
Who do you want, you snob, Peter O'Toole?

Ben Hur was good, maybe a little long.
Do you know that the author of *Ben Hur*,
Lew Wallace, was a Union general
and later governor of New Mexico?
The thing is, no one lived there then—nobody.
He was the governor of maybe twelve
Or thirteen guys—the governor of nothing!

When will I finish it, your Holiness?

I'm thinking I could make a little skylight
by banging my head against the ceiling, hard.

My Uncle's Bible

The pastel maps that show the Holy Land
are dimmer now. This rubber band is all
that holds the prophets back, who otherwise
flop out and sprawl along the floor like clowns.
My uncle was a navigator, killed
above the clouds, and when they mailed it back
with silver cufflinks and a wrinkled tie,

its binding was already torn and loose.
Had it been shot down too? My Grandma wondered.
She wasn't in the mood for metaphors.
Maybe my uncle damaged it himself;
he couldn't take it, not another raid
and, furious with terror, chucked his Bible,
cracking its spine against the barracks wall.

It may be time for me to chuck it too.
It's moldering. On somber days it looks
like it was wrested from a lunatic
or lodged by a tornado in a tree.
What could I swear to on its rotten hide?
This Good Book, yearning for oblivion,
the dump its long-awaited Kingdom Come.

Bangladesh

We have to start in 1965,
when all the gay meth heads couldn't decide
which one they most adored, Callas or Dylan,
both of them skinny as thermometers,
posing like sylphs in tight black turtlenecks.
Then, gradually, a multitude of Dylans

began to fill the park, croaking like frogs,
strumming guitars, blowing harmonicas,
hundreds and hundreds, several to a bench.
But there was only one Maria Callas,
sequestered in her gloomy Paris pad
and listening to Maria Callas records

(and nothing but), her bulky curtains closed,
which works for me because it worked for her.
What doesn't work is three David Lee Roths,
one checking bags at *Trash and Vaudeville*, one
strutting with ratted hair up St. Mark's Place,
and one zonked out in tights and on the nod,

surrounded by the Dylans in the park.
David Lee Roth times three would mean the times
would have to change, and so a roving band
of punk rockers began to beat the Dylans,
chasing them through the park and pounding them
senseless, then busting up their folk guitars

or stealing them. They even torture one
unlucky Dylan by the children's pool,
holding him down to burn him with Bic lighters,
then cackling when he begs to keep his Martin.
Later on at the precinct, deeply troubled,
a sensitive policeman contemplates

the crimes. Why were marauding gangs of punks
beating the Dylans in the park? He asks
himself, repeatedly, not realizing
that they, the punks, were cultural police
determined to eradicate the Dylans
and purify the park of Dylanesque

pollutions and corruptions, rank and abject
folk rock recrudescences, and worse —
that odious and putrid piety,
the sanctimoniousness of all the Dylans,
the phony holiness that peaks for Bob
(his faddish Christianity aside)

during the benefit for Bangladesh,
where George insists that Yoko not perform
and John agrees 'till Yoko blows her stack,
and they start primal-screaming at each other,
John flying out of JFK and nodding,
and Eric flying into JFK

and nodding. Well, Ravi would go on first,
the one and only Ravi Shankar, folks.
I saw him five times, three times high on acid,
the first time straight with Richard and his mom,
Debbie, who drove us down from Podunk High
to see him at the Syria Mosque (long gone,

bulldozed in '75). Debbie's not well.
Last August she was totally Alzheimered
and, my sweet lord, she made a pass at me,
which was embarrassing. Rebuffed but proud
she sat down on the porch swing with a thump,
and, chirping like a parakeet, she swung.

Stephen Duck and Edward Chicken

failed to make it into Schmidt's *Lives of the Poets*.
Duck, "The Thresher Poet of Pewsey Downs,"
would vault into the court of Caroline
and marry Sarah Big, her housekeeper.
"The Muse's Darling, Reverend Duck is dead,"
wrote Mary Collier, "The Poetical Washer-Woman,"
upon the unhappy event.
Also lamenting Duck were Henry Jones,
"The Poetical Bricklayer," and "Lactilla,
The Poetical Milkmaid of Clifton Hill."
Lactilla later wrote *The Royal Captives*,
an elephantine novel in five volumes,
which kept the wistful milkmaid at her desk
like a galley slave chained drooping to an oar.

I'd like to tell you more but Southey's splendid
Lives of the Uneducated Poets
is unavailable today from Bobst Library.
He made his pile off Valium, Elmer Bobst,
and that's just fine with me.
A Valium might have rescued Reverend Duck,
who drowned himself, Lord help us,
in a pond behind a rowdy, rustic tavern.
And while we're at it, pass the Valium, please,
to John Gould Fletcher (decades out of print),
who won the Pulitzer in '39,
drowned himself in a murky Ozark duck pond,
and failed, likewise, to make it into Schmidt.
He was rich, I think. Chicken was maybe a curate.

"The Poetical Bag-lady of Astor Place"
boards the 6 train and curses the entire car
for being "illiterate." "Spell mayonnaise,"
she hollers in my face. "Spell mayonnaise!"
And, discombobulated, I cannot.

The Treaty of Paris

1783

In this unfinished work by Benjamin West
our ministers are grouped off to the left,
and where, across from them, our vanquished foes,
the Brits, should be, there's just a misty blur.
Their envoys wouldn't sit, and so it seems
our ministers are meeting with a cloud.

It looks just like a Larry Rivers, too,
with Rothko pitching in (he did the cloud).
The painting's incompleteness can suggest
some metaphysical perplexities,
some problems that we might as well address.
The cloud could be a symbol, here, of absence,

a phantom delegation from the void,
or it might mean much more than that. The cloud
could be a metaphor for modern art
eating away the *ancien régime*
of neo-classicism. That explains it.
These foolish men, now styled our "founding fathers,"

have sold us down the river of abstraction.
The War of Independence—what a joke!
It was a blank, the shot heard 'round the world.
For surely it is they who must surrender,
John Jay, Ben Franklin, Adams, and the rest.
And what terms, after all, could they expect?

Those odious poltroons—they've sold us out!
That's not a treaty that they're signing. No!
It's utter and complete capitulation!
Those dunderheaded dolts, how dare they treat
with total vacancy? How dare they treat
with embassies of fog? So, now, we see

our flocks and herds, our mills and fisheries,
are stippled down in tiny specks and blotches
or swathed in deep and ever-darker hues.
Our people will dissolve. The weaker ones
will fade like ghosts into an atmosphere
where memory itself is brushed away.

Some will seek refuge in the Cubist missions.
Others will melt in surrealistic towns.
It can't be stopped. The very hand that guides
this pen is vanishing. It won't be me
in streaming rags, "escaped alone to tell thee."
It won't be me that gets you out of this.

The Searchers

Hangovers helped John Wayne evince deep torment
in *The Searchers*, when he comes unglued
while tracking the Comanches who've abducted
Natalie Wood. With Jeffrey Hunter as his
sidekick, he combs the empty wilderness
until the trail revolves into an odd

infinitude. The quest attains a sweeping,
cosmic grandeur as the wayworn pair
return repeatedly in Vista Vision
to bust up certain funerals and weddings,
while, past the stone pavilions of the canyon,
Natalie Wood still pines, a captive squaw.

Of course she's later rescued and returned,
and it's John Wayne who finally is forced
to drift along the dreary plain alone.
And Jeffrey Hunter (much beloved of Frank
O'Hara) went on to play the role of Christ,
as well as anyone has, in *King of Kings*,

where Nick Ray made him stay inside his trailer,
so he could smoke unseen by other cast
members, and extras would be awed by him
when he came on the set. Jeff shaved his armpits
for the Crucifixion, knowing well
the Lord must suffer in ideality,

mounted high and gleaming on the Cross,
a waxed and buff Apollo crowned with thorns.
It was the end, really, of Jeff's career,
banished to foreign features and depressed,
then suddenly dead at forty-three in obscure
circumstances, having fallen down a staircase.

Rose Poe

Rose Poe was homeless after Richmond fell,
abandoned by the millionaire MacKenzies,
whose ward she'd been for over fifty years.
She spent her days down at the railroad depot
trying to sell some faded photographs
of her unhappy brother, Edgar Allan,
now long deceased, the author of "The Raven."

His signature was forged across the portraits
in Rose's perfect hand. She had for years
taught penmanship to Richmond's "finest daughters"
at the MacKenzie's girls' academy.
She played piano, also, and gave lessons,
but many thought that she was rather dim,
including Edgar. She would sit up front
when Edgar read his poems, or gave a talk,
but then he'd tease her cruelly afterwards,
mocking the way she dressed and wore her hair
and remonstrating snappishly with her.

Her benefactors, too, could be unkind.
She had her room, her place at tea and table,
but they ignored her when she spoke, forgetting
at times, to introduce her to their guests.
She was a small and wren-like creature, Rose,
and she'd lost all her teeth in middle age,
and this embarrassed her so keenly, that,
increasingly, she kept herself apart.

* * *

When Lee retreated west to Appomattox
that spring, Rose Poe was left to stumble down
deserted boulevards in neighborhoods
that fires and explosions had destroyed,
places that she no longer recognized
they were so rubble-strewn.
                                          She couldn't sleep,
not in the overcrowded rectories,
and so she skulked around the homeless camps
alone, avoiding other indigents
(whom she disdained as her inferiors)
and always on the lookout for a place
where she'd feel safe.
                                Afraid of scavengers,
of convicts, dogs, deserters, drunks, and slaves,
now freed, she hid herself in alleyways,
which fear would people with a million phantoms.
So, helpless and forsaken, terrified
and hiding like a cat, Rose passed her nights,
a vagrant pauper in the conquered South.

* * *

Many of her aristocratic students
were desperate, too, and busy writing letters
to friends and relatives, writing in such
a lovely hand (for Rose had taught them well)
letters that pled for hidden jewels and heirlooms,
anything they could possibly sell or barter
to put some staples into empty cupboards.

For some were widows now with hungry children,
and some had husbands home with crippling wounds,
or husbands home, irascible and idle,
whittling sticks and moping in their yards.

* * *

On Sundays after church Rose would accost
acquaintances and beg them, frantically,
to let her come with them and sit a spell.
Some decent Christians took their turns relenting,
though usually her visits were a trial.
Rose strove so hard to please, reciting verse,
and, if they were unfortunate enough
to have a Steinway in their parlor, well,
Rose Poe could bang out hymns all afternoon.

Eventually, of course, they'd make her stop,
but then she'd pray enthusiastically,
not giving them a chance to interrupt,
chanting her supplications, crazed like some
mysteriarch who'd fallen from the moon
and landed accidently in Virginia,
an unacknowledged augeress, Rose Poe,
the soul or emblem of the ruined town.

Poor Collins

Poor Collins, near the end, a lunatic,
would claim he'd found the source of Shakespeare's *Tempest*
in a Spanish novel called *Aurelio*,
but when the Wartons asked to see the book,

he drew a map that led into the trees.
Poor Collins seldom left his mottled couch,
where he would often rave and "make great moanings,"
dying from melancholia, which was terminal

back then, at least for fey types like poor Collins.
Poor Collins reimbursed his publisher
for his unsold (and only) book of verse.
Then, like an idle felon flipping cards

into a hat, he stacked his books and flung
the whole edition in the fire. Poor Collins.
His sister Anne averred, glumly, that drink
had wrecked his nerves, but what unhinged poor Collins

was a horror of perdition. Now his name,
he feared, was blotted from the book of life,
and now his couch was just a grimy drum,
a rank mephitic chute into the wide

and gaping brimstone pit of Hell. Poor Collins,
condemned eternally, but for what sin?
Condemned for midnight trysts at Vauxhall Gardens?
Condemned for kissing Mrs. Cibber's hand?

Poor Collins, dosed with brandy by the spoon,
would even miss, at times, McDonald's madhouse,
especially when the tower bells rang down
to wig poor Collins out and set him spinning,

as dizzy as a dervish on his couch.
The unsung Pindar of his age, poor Collins,
a turbot flung up gasping hard, poor Collins.
A burly footman held him down, poor Collins.

Song of the Desert

With both the moon and Mercury in Pisces,
Nerval climbed up a ladder to the Sphinx
and jarred the idol into augury
by mumbling an Egyptian conjuration.

"Your uncle is the Emperor Napoleon,"
the Sphinx would say, or so Nerval would claim,
but, while his ladder teetered in the sand,
the pyramids stood crammed with mummy-runners

who made fake mummies out of real cadavers.
They lurked, these turbaned Igors, in the vaults,
where most fell prey to warring racketeers
and many wound up mummified themselves.

So, if you hear some singing, it's Radames
and Aida, warbling in their musty tomb,
while dying sacrificially for love.
Two-hundred grand, up front, the Pasha paid

to stage *Aida* at the Cairo opera.
There, Nubian slaves were played by Nubian slaves.
Give me the monumental lusciousness
of Dame Sophia Loren, stained Nubian,

our Technicolor, minstrel-show Aida,
who lipped, exquisitely, and with aplomb,
the delicate legato of Tebaldi.
And did she wiggle when she stood stock-still?

Let's say she stood there, tremblingly, demure;
she still could raise the Nile to inundation,
which overruns to drench the Memphian fields
and drain its cloudy sluice into the bay.

Playing his final Hamlet, Gielgud bombed,
completely, at the Cairo opera house.
Horatio had an epileptic fit
and fainted into Gielgud's velvet arms,

for starters. Then, the understudy, drunk,
lurched back and nearly tripped into the ghost.
"Look, my lord, it comes," he faintly bleated,
while pointing to the wrong end of the stage.

Confederates Try to Burn New York

November 1864

People had paid five bucks a seat that night
to catch all three Booth brothers in their togas.
Edwin, the brightest star, with Junius,
who'd recently become his Broadway rival,
and dastardly John Wilkes, the pale assassin,
who rode up on the train from Baltimore.

The Winter Garden Playhouse was so jammed
they had to put up benches in the aisles,
and, when a bottle of Greek fire flew
in from the street, a wild commotion spread
throughout the house. Edwin, alone on stage,
would calm the crowd while still in character,
exhorting them, sententiously, as Brutus,
to sit back down and disregard the hubbub.

Out strode John Wilkes who glared and crossed his arms,
aping the "Coriolanus" pose of Kemble.
The interruption aggravated him
because he had designs on Lucy Kane,
their pulchritudinous Calpurnia,
now fluttering offstage. No Antony
could slip the dogs of war like John Wilkes Booth,
with half as much flamboyancy and flare.
He knew she'd watch him from the wings, and knew
his brooding Antony would conquer her.

He didn't know Confederates had planned
to burn the city down, that very night,
around his ears. Eight rebel saboteurs
had registered in multiple hotels
and cased out targets like the Winter Garden
for maximum combustibility.

They started nineteen fires in an hour,
but most were minor blazes doused with ease.
(A traitor had diluted their Greek fire
the night before.) One lucky raider flung
a bottle into hay bales down at Barnum's,
and this flared up into a conflagration
that burned spectacularly for awhile.

Some animals from the menagerie
escaped in a stampede and, literally,
the mayhem in the streets became a circus.
An ostrich ran as far as Union Square,
and monkeys hid in St. Paul's Cemetery.
The Female Giant (over eight feet tall!)
loped down the street to Donnelley's Saloon,
anticipating whiskey on the house.

The rebels nonchalantly took the train
and, undetected, rode to Canada,
but one of them was caught, eventually,
crossing the border on his way back home
to Tennessee. They didn't hold him long.
That April he was hanged out in the harbor.

John Wilkes would fold his hand that April, also,
shot down inside a burning barn by Yankees,
who dragged him out still choking on his blood.
Five photographs of actresses fell out
of John Wilkes' coat, and these were rudely passed
around by men devoid of chivalry.

Inside the house, upstairs, another girl,
as lovely as those actresses, awoke,
and drawn out by the fire found a ruckus,
and Booth, disheveled, dying in the grass.
She knelt and held his lolling head awhile
to beautify this grand tableau, replete
with cavalry, this Viking funeral
without the boat. He died just after dawn,
somewhat romantically, I guess, but like
the man he shot, Booth was a fatalist,
and, "Useless, useless," were his final words.

Ronell Laborde

*The death, then, of a beautiful woman is, unquestionably,
the most poetical topic in the world. . . .* (Edgar Allan Poe)

We smoked and paced around the parking lot
at Cunningham's, my hometown funeral parlor,
and each of us took turns running for smokes.
We drove away, theatrically, but soon
returned at breakneck speeds to smoke and grieve
with rash exorbitance. Never have cars—
Fairlanes, Impalas, Galaxies, and Darts—
been polished like those cars were polished, then,
never, in automotive history.

Ronell Laborde had died at just fifteen,
stunning the town. She'd had rheumatic fever,
but nobody expected her to die.
They dressed her up to look like Sleeping Beauty,
the Disney version. Just exactly like her—
the blueness of her gown, the jeweled tiara,
the way they spread her hair across the pillow—
every single detail was the same.
Ronell was slender, blond, and beautiful,
and they had made her look like some cartoon,
a cartoon version of a fairytale.

It worked. A Disney Princess funeral
made perfect sense to us, and we all felt
that Mr. Cunningham had done his best.
He made us all come in. We couldn't smoke,

so sticks of gum were quickly passed around,
and everybody gawked at dead Ronell,
especially us, the teenage Edgar Poes,
who stood like suitors claiming suitor's rights;
because, conveniently enough, for us,
Ronell had died without a beau, and this
allowed us all to mourn her equally.

We couldn't breathe; there were so many flowers:
carnations, gladiolus, daffodils,
all stuffed around the casket in bouquets,
with babies' breath and white and yellow roses.

At last the organ started "In the Garden,"
my mother's favorite hymn. She'd fantasize
in church while singing it, imagining
herself among the lilies with the Lord.
Behind her back I had to laugh because
my mom had got so fat, it just seemed, well,
ridiculous to picture her that way,
sniffing the flowers with a glowing Jesus.

I couldn't picture that, or anything,
nor, for that matter, could my weeping friends,
that grief-ennobled troop of cavaliers.
Our young imaginations were demolished
completely, by that coffin's occupant;
I still can see her, after all these years.
Her skin was like cake frosting, only grayish,
and she was just as dead as dead can be.

Affair in Trinidad

Another *Gilda*'s what they tried to make,
so Glenn Ford sulked while Rita Hayworth danced,
and Alexander Scourby played the dirt-bag,
so slimily it boosted his career.
Ironically, Scourby is famous for
his unabridged recording of the Bible,
and blind believers have been harkening
to his sonority for sixty years.
It's still the best complete King James recording.

He wasn't necessarily that pious,
Scourby, not quite the missionary type,
but, later he was asked to narrate *Jesus*,
the movie, which bombed badly here at home,
but elsewhere has been viewed six billion times,
in countries undeveloped and remote,
by many who had never seen a film
before.
            Two hundred million souls were brought
into the fold—two hundred million souls!

In deep and steamy jungle glades they knelt
to take, from dented chalices, communion,
and villagers in Chinese catacombs
with blubbered cheeks sang hymns before the Cross.

But when we watch *Affair in Trinidad*
it's Rita that concerns us most, let's face it.
She's gotten harder and she's stiffened too;
the favorite partner of Astaire has stiffened,
not much, but it's not difficult to notice.
Her shoulders and her elbows aren't as supple.
She was an alcoholic and a smoker,
who'd had two kids. But that's not it, not really.
She just felt disappointed, constantly,
and had a lot of serious complaints.

Her womanizing husbands, let's start there.
The prince turned out to be (surprise!) a playboy,
and Orson would audition younger "talent."
His host of brilliant friends were not so brilliant,
either, and most of them were on the make
like everybody else in Hollywood.

And if she went alone out to a party,
or tried to get a snootful in a club, well,
producers and associate producers
wanted to dance, wanted to rub themselves
a little bit on Rita.
                    Harry Cohn,
meanwhile, refused to hear her grievances,
giving her dopey roles with dopey dances.

That hardened her and so she took up painting,
and met a whole new mob of dilettantes,
to mix in with the Malibu riffraff
and wannabes. Those minions who had minions,
those creatures who had creatures, those musclemen
and manikins who radiated pain—
they stiffened her.
                    They crowded in at parties,
forcing her favorites out onto the terrace,
the xylophonists and ventriloquists
who lived in cheap hotels, cosmographers,
well used to heavy seas, the devotees
of Dionysus, frantic for the hour
when Rita danced the dance of seven veils.

Jeffers' *Medea* Opens on Broadway with Judith Anderson

October 20, 1947

Dame Judith took a dozen curtain calls
before the cry of "Author, author," rose,
insistently, to where the poet sat
with Una, in the dark, shyly exulting.
She prodded him until he finally stood

and awkwardly accepted their applause.
He would have trampled over all of them
to get a double scotch and a Pall Mall,
but he felt glad and vindicated, too,
for proving that Euripides could sing

in loosely wrought accentual English verse.
A few days earlier, during rehearsals,
poking around backstage he'd found some stairs
and thought he'd go exploring in the basement.
He stopped halfway. A multitude of rats,

a colony, were scampering hell-bent
across the floor. Construction down the block
had stirred them up, and Jeffers was amazed
and, though he wouldn't have confessed it, scared.
It was sublime, that sea of rippling fur

flowing beneath the stage where Judith ranted.
But what could they be heralding, he wondered?
Some downfall, surely, some complete disaster.
Well, those misgivings would evaporate
in copious applause—they had a hit,

a smash in fact—every review was good.
The highbrows and the eggheads ate it up.
With Judith as the wicked witch who kills
her kids to make a point, how could they lose?
Jeffers flew home in triumph to Carmel

but soon became morose up in his tower,
sulking for days and drinking like a pirate,
while downstairs, Una, aggravated, bumped
the ceiling with a broom, berating him
for sottish, gross, ungrateful cussedness.

Then *Life* came out and gave them two whole pages
with shots of Judith, Jeffers, and John Gielgud
(who played a nervous Jason and directed).
For toppers, Richard Boone was in the cast,
our existential cowboy cavalier.

I love the end of *Hombre*, when he asks
Paul Newman, "What do you suppose that hell
is gonna look like?" Paul replies, "We've all
got to die, it's just a question of when."
Then both men draw and shoot each other dead.

Tarzan and the Leopard Woman

Back in the fifties, Gordon Scott was Tarzan,
the buffest ape-man yet in Technicolor
but just a little priggish for the part.
His grammar was correct—a fatal flaw.
He seemed more like a sculptor from Big Sur.

The only jungle lord who really mattered
was Weissmuller, the Nureyev of Tarzans,
who dove, undaunted, off the Brooklyn Bridge
and off the highest cliff in Acapulco.
Sadly his middle age waxed sore on him,

causing his pecs to flap after he jumped
onto a branch, and so they put him in
a shirt and made him Jungle Jim. He never
could get away from jungle roles. "Boy," too,
got trapped—as Bomba in the serials.

Maureen O'Sullivan got out, however,
and writers had to try to kill "Jane" off
with poison darts or natural disasters,
but fans protested, so she went to "London"
instead, addressing all her cablegrams

to *Tarzan of the Apes*. This opened up
a secret passageway deep in the jungle,
through which the hotter chorus girls would slink
to fill the Jane-void temporarily:
Blond hoochy-koochy harems from Mogambo

and maenads from the Shah of Timbuktu,
all twirling in high heels and Kismet clothes,
while Tarzan, undistracted, saves the treasure
and hurls the wizard into bubbling muck.
Riding an elephant, the wanton heiress

flees, anxious to avoid those nymphs, who, in
their long processionals can complicate
the night on high plateaus. There, beneath
the broken colonnades, the pin-up vestals
file past the ruined Temples of the Moon.

The Death of Winckelmann

Trieste 1768

I.

The Abbé Winckelmann was at his desk
in the hotel, when his new friend Francesco
returned, ostensibly in search of his
dropped handkerchief. He asked to see, once more,
the special medals from Her Holy Empress,
and Winckelmann obliged him merrily
by waving them like censers in the air.
Done with his "fair Antinous" charade,
Francesco made his move and pulled a knife,
intent on robbery. A fight ensued,
and Winckelmann was stabbed at least five times.
Some servant, hearing cries, surprised the thief,
who fled, with gory hands, into the street
and hid himself nearby inside a shed.
The Abbé staggered to the balcony,
pressing a cloth against his streaming wounds.

II.

He'd argued that the turbulent *Laocoön*
embodied chaste decorum and restraint.
Sedateness was a virtue in itself,
for this bookish son of an epileptic cobbler.
Gripping the banister, he had become
a grisly simulacrum of the statue,
peering in desperation, faintly, down
into the dim and cavernous hotel.
A bustling group of servants mounted toward
him on the stairs, some shrieking in their panic,
until they reached him finally and hushed,
stopping to catch their breath before they tipped
him gently down onto a mattress. Then,
as though he truly were a wounded king
or holy martyr, some fell on their knees,
while some like saints or ancient Romans stood
and hid their pallid faces in their hands.

III.

Poor Winckelmann had met his murderer
only the week before. Francesco heard
him asking about ships, and, butting in,
told Winckelmann that he knew of a captain
whose brigantine was ready to embark.
The two men set out for the quay but went
instead to a coffeehouse where both indulged
forbidden inclinations. They returned
to the hotel and were inseparable
thereafter, although both were unforthcoming.
The Abbé served as Papal Antiquary
and never told his friend. Francesco failed,
for his part, to disclose that he had just
been freed from jail. He thought the Abbé was
a spy or an adventurer, perhaps
a Lutheran or a Jew. At any rate,
there by himself, with money, in Trieste,
he made an easy mark for young Francesco.
The scholar had been frantic to persuade
his *amoroso* to return with him
and foolishly showed off a golden snuffbox,
a gift from the Marquis of Tavistock.

IV.

He'd hoped to die held in the broken arms
of his beloved Apollo Belvedere
and glide through heaven pressed to that pure stone.
But now a guardsman thumbed his battered *Iliad*,
while a condoling monk assisted him
in drawing up a will, which he would die
trying to sign. Francesco, on the wheel,
would bawl and beg for death, then lie exposed
as fare for famished dogs and harbor fowl.
A courier, dispatched to Rome, would bring
the awful tidings to the Vatican.
Cassandra-like, Frau Kaufmann went to Mass,
and, trudging through the galleries, distraught,
Mengs wept before the Barberini Faun.
The medals were discovered by a cardinal,
uncatalogued, among the Abbé's things.

V.

We have our own Apollo Belvedere,
which Winckelmann inspired, at the Met.
A grand Canova on the balcony,
of Perseus rampant with the baleful head.
The victor with his magic shoes and helmet
is otherwise stark naked in the court
of Polydectes, where he hoists his trophy,
high and dripping, up before the hall,
to petrify the whole licentious rout
and end the tyrant's terrible misrule.
The scene, at last, was what the gods had wished.
Our hero rode through town, pelted with flowers,
while pageants overspread the countryside.
Danaë rejoiced, the Nereids rejoiced,
Andromeda rejoiced in broken chains,
for Perseus had delivered up the palace
and greeted faithful Dictus with the crown.

The Magnificent Frigatebird

They're bullies and the way they feed is gross,
forcing the smaller fishers to disgorge
their catch in flight, then swooping down to snatch
it for themselves. Along the beach they court
in gangs, frenetically, lacking the charm
of strolling balladeers. Absurdly they
all clack their curious bills and flap their wings,
fluttering for the females overhead,
who then fly off with them to strange lagoons.
Honeymoons there are brief because the males,
like feathery Casanovas, soon decamp,
eager for more romance, stranding their mates,
who contemplate the need to nest alone
in what magnificence the marsh affords.

Pavarotti Gala at the Met

We had concerns. He was so huge his tux
looked like a tent, and, now, supposedly,
both knees were shot. Lately he'd sing a role,
like Chénier, sitting down, sitting or propped
up by some scenery. He'd even sit
through duels and arias, and carpenters
in every house had customized their *Toscas*,
so he could do the whole show on his duff.

The worst bit was the water. They hid cups
around the set, so he could slyly turn
his hefty back on us and take a slurp.
He'd sneak off stage to wet his whistle, too,
eliciting, at times, derisive laughter.
Once he crept off in Act II of *Un Ballo*,
leaving the flabbergasted Deborah Voight
alone on stage, stranded in mid-duet,
the king of Sweden summoned off, by whom
no one could say.
                    The hats and scarves got worse,
and then, Lord help us, Sting and Bono came
with all the scrawny, barefoot Balkan orphans
begging for bread, pulling him in his clown clothes
deeper and deeper into Yanni-land.

* * *

A wounded angel is an angel still,
we'd like to think, and, luckily for us,
June Anderson was there with him on stage
that afternoon. Her supernatural voice
would harmonize delightfully with his,
and he came through on every aria,
pellucidly. His voice, though darker, bloomed
for us with all its former plangency
restored, and we were stupefied with joy,
like kids with cotton candy at the circus.
But his anxieties were palpable, as well,
the way he kissed June's forehead desperately
during applause, as though he'd just survived
a mine collapse, hugging her hard because
the pain he felt was not just in his knees.

Compulsiveness had called the shots too long,
and he was far too arrogant to change,
although attempts, however ineffectual
and brief, were made.
                      But, anyhow, his voice,
that day, was burgeoning, and certainly
we all were thrilled, in our expensive seats,
to hear those lambent tones again that can
release us into some Elysium
of song, dispelling temporarily, at least,
the gloom of apprehension and regret.

To a Young Girl in Washington Square Park

Lolling beneath the Garibaldi statue,
you look like some pre-Raphaelite Cordelia,
except you're tarted up for rock and roll.
Your beauty is the barrel you'll go over

the falls in, and you're copping now, I see—
I hope it's only pot. Oh I would row
you back to Astolat, and swiftly too,
but that's just not my job. You're on your own,

and while you gambol off to get your buzz,
the statue tries to pull its damaged sword,
snapped off by hooligans eons ago.
That sword reminds me now of Marshal Ney,

who charged at Waterloo with half a saber
brandished above his powder-blackened head.
Five horses fell from under him, before,
unscathed, he made it out, at last, on foot,

only to find disaster on the roads,
and gallantry in short supply; though he
would tramp along, apparently unshaken,
to Paris and a Bourbon firing squad.

Hartley Coleridge

Drunk as a tick and lost out in a storm,
the younger Coleridge couldn't find his road
and fell so many times his pants were ripped
out at the knees. He'd roamed too far again
and had too many pints, and, foolishly,
although his friends insisted that he stay,
he'd set out under heavy clouds for home.

The Wordsworths worried chronically and blamed
his father's irresponsibility
for Hartley's shiftless ways. For what had Samuel
bequeathed his son besides an aptitude
for verse—an aptitude for sottishness
and misery? "My babe so beautiful
it thrills my heart," he gushed with mawkish pride,
before he vanished like a sorcerer
to eat the lotus in his Highgate den.

I don't think we should blame his father, though;
courting is what would damage "little Hartley."
He was preposterously odd and short,
so short the girls would call him Rumpelstiltskin
and mock him, constantly, behind his back.

He tried to compensate by sonneteering,
composing poems for girls he'd glimpsed, just once,
out on the lake, the ones who waved from boats
as they sailed by. He'd versify as well
for girls in shops, the ones who hid from him

and tittered audibly from dressing rooms,
the ones who'd hand his sonnets back unread.
And so he would carouse around the lakes,
hiking for miles to drink in distant taverns,
sleeping in barns and sometimes in a ditch
beside the road.
                    So there were times like these,
lost in the storm, when he seemed doomed. In fact,
this time he was. He recognized, at last,
a neighbor's house and took a cowpath home,
where his two dogs were barking, anxiously.
The rain had failed to sober him, and Hartley
forgot to light the stove. He fell asleep
in soaking clothes and, well, that was the end.
He got so sick and in a fever died.

Wordsworth was overcome and couldn't bear
to see the grave. He never understood
the dissipation and the lassitude,
and Hartley's inability to cope.

The worst thoughts and the worst words, too, all in
the worst of orders, that's what Hartley had
to go with breakfast there at Rydal Water,
and just as much as anyone back then
he listened hard to spirits and to nature.

But was that really such a good idea?
For years of dedicated tippling meant
that Hartley's brain was soft, and he could be
ensorcelled by a specter or the wraith
of some drowned girl, who, wrapped up in the mist
would lead him lost half way to Windemere
on roads that looked deceptively familiar.

Broad Stripes and Bright Stars

It was a joyful noise unto the Lord
that Hendrix made that morning, smelting down
the National Anthem. He did a Motown saraband
and roused the bleary throng of lotus eaters

so gallantly streaming there in the Woodstock pasture.
The gang at the v.f.w. was not amused,
preferring a traditional arrangement
of the peppy trumpet march turned drinking song

first known as "To Anacreon in Heaven."
Enter Francis Scott Key, the lawyer-poet,
perched in the rigging of a British sloop,
an overdressed envoy gesticulating

like a tenor toward the bombed fort and snapping flag,
his verses coming in a vatic trance
to be scribbled later on an envelope.
All night on deck Doc Beane had paced and nattered,

"Is our flag still there?" It was, and Key's poetastery
was soon sung out by choirs across the land.
But the President and his bewildered cabinet
had gathered like rambling gypsies on a hilltop,

the better to behold their smoking capital,
and Dolly Madison, disguised as a farmwife,
wandered in a wagon, up and down the roads,
for two days nearly lost in the countryside.

On the Removal of the Auden Plaque from 77 St. Mark's Place

When Pindar's town was burnt by Alexander
the poet's heirs were all left safe indoors.
Entrepreneurs thought St. Mark's could be grander
and gutted Wystan's house to add more floors.

Grand, smoky parties, Flagstad in hi-fi,
a car assigned to drive Miss Moore back home—
it might as well have happened in Shanghai;
they've taken down the marker and the poem.

The bar survived next door where he would go
unbathed and rumpled with the *Times'* crossword,
and at that idle toil he would know
the pity in the prattle overheard.
The pity of this house—his missing name.
The landlords and the city are to blame.

Art in America

They had been drinking, heavily, all night,
mostly champagne. They watched the U.S. Open,
the Yankee game, "The Son of Dracula,"
and "Without Love," a Tracy-Hepburn classic,
which lit a fuse somehow—they started fighting.
Fed-up with all his phony promises
to help with her career, and armed with proof

of his persistent infidelity,
she asked for a divorce. That's when he flipped
because he'd married her without a pre-nup.
Champagne was spilled, a chair was overturned,
some empty bottles rolled along the floor.
At five a.m., or thereabouts, it stopped:
She "tumbled" out the window of their high-rise.

It was a muggy night, and she was wearing
only a pair of blue bikini panties.
So, drunk and nearly naked, out she went
into the clammy air, falling so far
that all her bones were smashed. She also dented,
deeply, the rooftop of the deli where
she landed. That was the ironic part—

the dent. For she did "body art" and made
impressions in the sand shaped like her body.
Lying in them, she'd photograph herself
naked, and naturally these "pieces" looked
like sandy little monsters, fetuses
that would prefigure, paradoxically,
the gruesome imprint made by her collision.

He was the famous one, the one who sold
the Tate a pile of rocks, a pompous fraud
and doyen of the sand-box school, now doomed
to be the OJ of the galleries.
But she's the one who liked to mess with it.
To mess, theatrically, with craziness.
I drank with her; I saw her voodoo act,

her Santeria ritual of blood.
She ululated and she cast her spells,
joking at first, until it wasn't funny
so much as desperate, but she invoked
those demons that came back to snatch her later.
Her work went up in value instantly
when she became, for the "Guerilla Girls,"

a martyr. That would be the biggest joke—
her feminism. She might fake it sometimes
when women were around, or when it served
her huge ambition. That's the only thing
she cared about. It's all so obvious
and typical. It's why she married him
and why I can't feel sorry for her now.

Oh sure, she loved that ogre, and she loved
his overalls; there's lots of love like that,
here in this town. There're lots of hustlers, too,
who desecrate the arts, and, more and more,
they rise to prominence. But none of them
could make it here, or even get a show,
unless the scene was absolutely rotten.

Repairs Delay Discovery Launch Again

After the Challenger disaster, Brodsky
would eulogize the crew, claiming that they
had "left the vivid air signed with their honor,"
a stirring bit of Spender quoted in,

I fear, poor taste, because one can't help picturing
the shuttle lost in flames, and flames won't do
as "signature" for those departed souls.
Since the Columbia blew up last year,

I've wondered, morbidly, if any of
the astronauts died badly—a quaintly apt
expression, as in, "Dr. Johnson was
afraid of dying badly." I don't expect

an astronaut would lose control completely.
They put them through so many grueling tests.
I know they wouldn't scream like Aunt Loretta,
careening on the Coney Island Cyclone.

But, still, the end at hand, a pilot may
have prayed too fervently, spitting some spray,
by accident onto a crewmate who
was busy telepathing his farewell

down to his frantic wife in Florida.
Now, I'm the prayerful, spraying type, myself,
and hope the soul survives its fleshly mansion,
but when you're vaporized in burning gas

and then dissolved in freezing space, I have
to wonder how your soul could fly away
from that. No one would go contentedly
into a state of punishment, said Johnson,

or pass contentedly into oblivion.
We must repose our faith in God, Amen.
Well, Johnson preached his sermon in a longboat
with lairds to pull the oars en route to Skye.

Imagine him bewigged and gravy-stained,
on a rocket primed to blow itself to atoms.
Would Johnson stand, Horatius-like, undaunted,
to meet the fatal blast at mach-eighteen?

I think he would, for he was often brave
and even venturesome. Warned that a gun
would burst if overloaded, he nonchalantly
rammed in several balls and fired it off;

and when, one night, four goons accosted him,
he smacked the leading malefactor down
and monkey-stomped the sorry bastard, keeping
the rest at bay until the watch came up.

One-Ring Circus, 1960

The elephants looked languid on parade,
all three of them, under the not-so-Big-Top,
the one top of this hayseed-circuit circus
that shambled into town. Kids would get stuck
for hours on the broken Ferris wheel,
while gold-toothed barkers rooked the local rubes
out of their dimes.
             The lions wouldn't leap,
and crippled midgets vexed decrepit clowns
in sweltering July humidity,
but dairy farmers clap when they are cued
by bows and flourishes.
             The only thrill
came when a bareback rider rode through flames,
a pretty girl but puffy for her age,
no doubt from drink, though all of them looked like
they lived on hotdogs.
             The aerialists above
would pose compulsively, filled with the false
vitality of studied decadence,
a threadbare robe flung on impoverishment,
a doomed tradition wheezing in the sticks.

The sideshow tents were worse. Repugnant geeks
still lurked, and wan hermaphrodites revolved
on creaking pillories. That year I saw
"The Largest Python in Captivity."
It roasted under glass, captive and dead.

Lepanto

Our bigger galleasses and bigger guns
would blow the sultan's navy into kindling,
but combat was ferocious on all sides.
Captain Venusta had his hand blown off
and shoved his smoking stump into a hen,
fighting on fiercely with that squawking muff

until he fell beneath a bristling cloud
of arrows. Boarders stormed the pasha's ship
and jammed his severed head onto a pole,
which admirals handed on from cheering deck
to cheering deck. Everywhere you looked
the Turks were in retreat or in the water.

Our knights, berserk with rage, speared them with pikes
and clobbered them with oars, while cannoneers,
at close range, blew them off the crowded spars
they floated on. Those that swam off were drowned.
Their galley slaves, unchained, began to bawl
in unison, praying aloud to Mary,

whose intercession, everyone agreed,
had granted victory. The Ottomans
had, temporarily, been beaten back,
and galleys, guns, and chests of gold were seized.
We took a ton of sequins from their flagship,
and every bell in Christendom was rung.

* * *

Cervantes, wounded three times, nearly died,
and, luckily, his left hand had been mangled,
which saved him from a slow death in the galleys.
The Moors would hold him captive for five years,
but, even after three escape attempts,
they let him stroll at leisure on the beach.

Waiting for ransom, he beguiled his captors
with palm-readings and astrological
prognostications, helping them resolve
disputes, while scheming, desperately, for food.
Barefoot, in rags, he paced around the fort
and wrote his verses in a crumbling tower;

wrote them by memory, wrote them in sand,
to keep a tenuous hold on fading powers.
Watching the sea until he thought the sea
was watching him, he lost all track of time,
dreaming of indecipherable books
and monsters that his sword could never wound.

Back home, he took great pride in his survival
and knew those years of wrangling with corsairs,
those years of starving on the beach, had taught
him more than patience in adversity.
He could, at will, dissolve into the ether,
dissolve into the empty golden shore.

Yeats Takes Up Fencing at Forty

and Ezra snickers up his velvet sleeve,
swords having been hurled into the pit:
Brave Roland's Durandel with St. Peter's tooth
enclosed in its hilt, and the Cid's Tizona
worth more than a thousand silver marks.
Oh for a fresh sword to hew Agag in pieces!
A ringing blade from Errol Flynn or Tyrone Power
wielded by torchlight against the master, Basil Rathbone,
on the stairways of the usurper's palace
or in the hall of the perfidious Alcalde.
Poor Tyrone, troubled and dissolute,
dropped dead from a heart-attack sword fighting
George Sanders in *Solomon and Sheba*,
the love scenes with The Lollobrigida incomplete.
"You are the White Goddess," Robert Graves told her.
Mosby thought that sabers belonged in museums
and rode with the Iliad in his saddle-bags.
His men went on their night-raids armed with pistols,
hiding their wounded in cellars and barns.
Mosby hid himself, once, high in a shivering oak,
while cursing Federals searched the house
and the wind made its ocean in the leaves.

The Martian Translation

One of the 9th Street bums is cracking up,
beet-faced, wet-brained, wool coat in July;
he's doing a Martian translation
of speeches from Shakespeare.

First, Timon-like, he curses
the entire town, brick and mortar.
Then he's Macbeth, talking horror to his hands,
and Othello bawling softly over

the bride he'll have to suffocate.
For an encore he does Richard
spinning and shrieking on Bosworth Field.
Anon, the light changes and I cross the street,

but an hour later he's still there,
bumping the pocked wall,
settled now, like a fly on a window pane.
Well, he's not going to let me pass unbothered,

and so he totters, genuflects and begs.
And don't I dig deep?
Glad to arrest bewilderment
and cast it back into oblivion.

Little Cross

My father carried a little cross
in his pocket with his change.
It couldn't have been silver.
Nothing my parents owned
was very valuable.
Their bath towels were so cheap
they'd barely dry you.

Blind, he could only
feel the cross in his palm
and showed it to me just once,
quietly, to celebrate my return
from the pigpen to Methodism.
His Calvary would last four years —
performing the Stations of the Cross
in his pajamas — on a loop.

The Imam grew angry at the Christians
who said that good things come from God
and bad things from Mohammed,
when all things come from God.

My father dying with his mouth frozen
wide open like a baby chick
(because if you don't fix the mouth
the undertaker has to saw it shut)
and not dying in his pajamas —
his pajamas on the other guy,
mixed up by the laundry in the home.

And spring came early this year
with Stinky the Dog
and Whore, a little junkie barf in her hair,
good body but buck teeth,
from no one buying the braces.